I0821115

You Are Invited

THAT HOLY WEEK SO LONG AGO

The Seven Days That Led to Easter

Written by
MATTHEW BOSWELL

Illustrated by
HELENA PEREZ GARCIA

CROSSWAY®
WHEATON, ILLINOIS

That Holy Week So Long Ago: The Seven Days That Led to Easter

Published by Crossway
1300 Crescent Street
Wheaton, Illinois 60187

Illustrations, book design, and cover design: Helena Perez Garcia

First printing 2026

Printed in China

Hardcover ISBN: 979-8-8749-0099-1

Library of Congress Cataloging-in-Publication Data

Names: Boswell, Matthew, 1979– author | Pérez García, Helena illustrator

Title: The Holy Week so long ago : the seven days that led to Easter / Matthew Boswell ; illustrated by Helena Perez Garcia.

Description: Wheaton, Illinois : Crossway, 2026

Identifiers: LCCN 2025023788 | ISBN 9798874900991 (hardcover)

Subjects: LCSH: Holy Week—Juvenile literature | LCGFT: Literature

Classification: LCC BT414 .B67 2026 | DDC 242/.35—dc23/eng/20250820

LC record available at https://lccn.loc.gov/2025023788

Crossway is a publishing ministry of Good News Publishers.

RRDS 36 35 34 33 32 31 30 29 28 27 26
15 14 13 12 11 10 9 8 7 6 5 4 3 2 1

For Caden, Avery, Addy, and Cannon

–Matthew

For my mum

–Helena

You Are Invited

THE INVITATION OF HOLY WEEK

The events of Holy Week are more than just moments in a story. They show the extraordinary lengths God went to in order to save us from our sin and to display his glory. This true story announces truly good news!

This special week also invites you to become part of the story. We hear the invitation in the first words of Jesus's public ministry recorded in the Gospel of Mark: "The time is fulfilled, and the kingdom of God is at hand; repent and believe in the gospel" (Mark 1:15).

As you read about Holy Week, I hope you see the glory and grace of King Jesus as never before. The one who gave his life invites you into a life of repenting of your sin and believing in him as your Savior. Even today, a holy Savior still creates a holy people through the events of that Holy Week so long ago.

THE STORY OF HOLY WEEK

That Holy Week so long ago,
Each day helps tell the story
Of Jesus Christ who lived and died,
Then rose again in glory.
Some days that week were sad and bleak,
Yet if you keep on reading,
You'll hear how sweet the gospel rings
With news that's worth repeating.

PALM SUNDAY

The first Palm Sunday, Jesus rode
Upon a donkey seated;
The humble Christ came into town
With palms and praises greeted.
Both young and old began to sing
Of wondrous works he'd done:
"Hosanna, loud hosannas bring
To bless the promised one."

HOLY MONDAY

On Holy Monday, fearlessly
In front of all to see,
The Christ cleared out some temple thieves,
Then cursed a fruitless tree.
The lesson of the tree was this:
That fruit should mark our way.
The lesson of the temple is—
God welcomes us to pray.

HOLY TUESDAY

On Holy Tuesday, people asked
About God's word and rules.
So Jesus answered and he used
Great stories as his tools.
He told them God's entire law,
Divided in two parts:
They first must love the Lord their God,
Then neighbors from their hearts.

SPY WEDNESDAY

Throughout Spy Wednesday Jesus taught
The people in the light.
While Judas schemed in shadows deep—
A plan by dark of night.
Just thirty silver pieces was
The price set to betray
The King of all who came in love
To take our sins away.

MAUNDY THURSDAY

On Maundy Thursday Jesus washed
His dear disciples' feet.
He spoke to them of things to come
A work almost complete.
One final time they all enjoyed
The old Passover meal.
He blessed the cup and broke the bread,
A covenant to seal.

GOOD FRIDAY

On grim Good Friday, on a hill
The Lamb laid down his life;
The sinless one for sinners slain,
The perfect sacrifice.
A cross of wood became the sign—
Here grace so brightly shown.
The death of death Christ died to win:
Salvation for his own.

HOLY SATURDAY

On quiet Holy Saturday,
Beside the massive stone,
Fierce guards stood watch so ev'ryone
Would leave the grave alone.
Within the tomb in linen cloths
The King lay slain by death,
His body still and motionless—
No sight, no sound, no breath.

But . . .

RESURRECTION SUNDAY

As Resurrection Sunday broke,
With brilliance more than light,
Up from the grave the Son arose
To end the endless night.
Defeating Satan, conquering sin,
Removing death's cold sting—
He lives to give eternal life,
Our resurrected King.

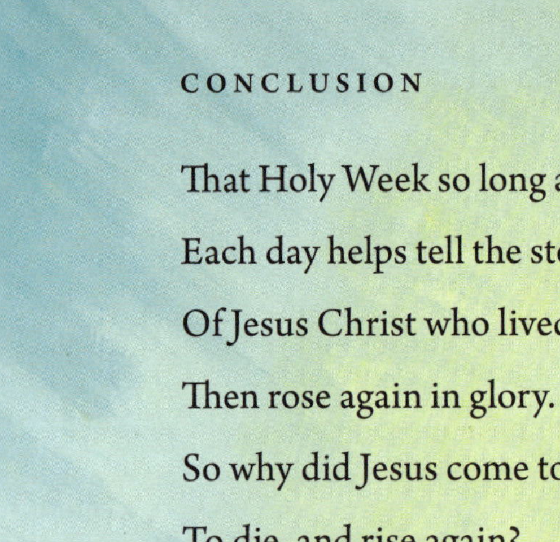

CONCLUSION

That Holy Week so long ago
Each day helps tell the story
Of Jesus Christ who lived and died,
Then rose again in glory.
So why did Jesus come to live,
To die, and rise again?
To show the love of God above,
To save us from our sin.

HOLY WEEK

HOLY WEEK BEGINS with Palm Sunday and ends with Holy Saturday. (Resurrection Sunday stands as its own special event.) Both Sundays are glorious, yet the six days in between are not easy. The cross came before the crown. This one week so long ago held some of the most important events of the Christian faith—namely, the death and resurrection of Jesus Christ. That is why it is known as Holy Week.

ON PALM SUNDAY, Jesus rode into Jerusalem seated on a donkey, fulfilling the prophecy from Zechariah 9:9. He was greeted by a joyful crowd shouting, "Hosanna!" ("Save us, we pray!") and praising him as their Savior. We call this day Palm Sunday because the people celebrated by waving palm branches as he rode past and by laying them on the road ahead of him to honor his arrival.

ON HOLY MONDAY, Jesus entered the Jerusalem temple and was upset when he saw people making it difficult for others to worship God. (This is the famous scene where he turned over the tables of people selling things.) Earlier in the day, Jesus cursed a fruitless fig tree, which, by the next morning, had withered. We call this day Holy Monday, to group it with the other days of Holy Week.

ON HOLY TUESDAY, Jesus taught people in the temple using stories called parables. (He often taught this way.) The leaders tried to trap him with tricky questions, but he answered them wisely. Jesus explained God's kingdom and the future to them. We call this day Holy Tuesday to count down the days until Jesus's death and resurrection.

ON SPY WEDNESDAY, Jesus continued teaching the people in parables, while Judas quietly made a deal with the religious leaders to betray him. We call this day Spy Wednesday to describe the secret actions of Judas. He went to the leaders and offered to show them where Jesus would be when the crowds were not around—for a price. They agreed to pay Judas thirty pieces of silver.

ON MAUNDY THURSDAY, Jesus shared the Last Supper with his disciples. He washed their feet as an act of love and service, instructing them to remember him whenever they ate the Lord's Supper in the future. We call this day Maundy Thursday because on this night Jesus gave his disciples a new command: to love one another as he had loved them (John 13:34). Maundy is shorthand for the Latin word *mandatum*, which means "command." Later that night, Jesus went to a garden to pray, where Judas betrayed him with a kiss.

ON GOOD FRIDAY, Jesus was unjustly arrested, mockingly tried, swiftly sentenced, and brutally crucified. So why would anyone ever refer to this day as "good"? The answer is that, because of what happened on that day, sinners can now receive eternal good. Through Jesus's death, forgiveness of sins was secured once and for all, making it possible for all who trust in him by faith to receive salvation.

ON HOLY SATURDAY, Jesus's body was placed in a tomb, and a massive stone was placed in front to seal it shut. Roman soldiers guarded the grave; no one could tamper with the body. Jesus's friends were sad and scared. They huddled together to grieve the loss of their Lord.

THE REPORTS OF RESURRECTION SUNDAY begin with women who visited Jesus's tomb. There they found the stone rolled away and the tomb empty. An angel told them Jesus was alive! Jesus then appeared to his friends and showed them he had risen from the dead, bringing them great joy and hope. In many places this day is called Easter, but for a long time it has been called Resurrection Sunday—a day set aside to celebrate the good news of the resurrection of Jesus Christ.

NOTE TO PARENTS

That Holy Week So Long Ago recounts the events during the final days of Jesus's life and ministry on earth. This week holds profound significance. It begins with Jesus's triumphal entry into Jerusalem, where crowds wave palm branches and greet him with shouts of "Hosanna!" And it culminates in his stunning triumph over Satan, sin, and death. The climactic beginning and conclusion of this week transform the entire week from a series of events into moments imbued with eternal meaning.

Each year, Holy Week comes and goes with many believers remaining unaware of the deep importance of the days leading up to Jesus Christ's death and resurrection. My goal in writing a rhyming book for children is to both educate youngsters and engage parents, helping both groups cultivate a richer understanding of these pivotal days.

Each turn of the page highlights a different day of Holy Week, from Palm Sunday to Resurrection Sunday. Some days are familiar to us. On Palm Sunday, Jesus's entrance into Jerusalem sets the tone for the coming days; it's a scene filled with joy and expectation. Holy Monday sees him clearing the temple, emphasizing the sanctity of worship. On Maundy Thursday, the Last Supper provides not only a lesson and a meal but also a new covenant that demands the very life of Christ. Good Friday brings sorrow and solemn reflection, as Jesus's crucifixion reveals the depth of his sacrifice. Other days are less familiar, with less familiar events and names (like Holy Tuesday and Spy Wednesday). Yet all the days of this week are key for understanding the full narrative of salvation.

As a father whose children are quickly stretching into adulthood, I wrote this book with them in mind. I wanted them to understand, even in their teenage years, the unshakable tenets of our faith—truths that have shaped our family and, I pray, will continue to shape each of them throughout their lives. I aimed to create a resource that would make the events of Holy Week accessible and memorable for both young readers and their parents.

By reading each page together, families can explore these significant days, sparking conversations that deepen their faith and understanding. This book is a heartfelt tool designed to bring the generations together and ensure that the meaning of Holy Week is not lost but celebrated and cherished year after year.

You Are Invited
You Are Invited
You Are Invited

You Are Invited
You Are Invited
You Are Invited